Mel Bay's

HARMONICA
Pocket Companion

Great songs for fun, camping, backpacking, floating, and pleasure.

By Bill Bay

1 2 3 4 5 6 7 8 9 0

CONTENTS

PROPER POSITION

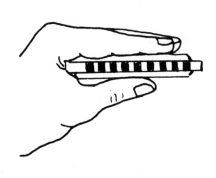

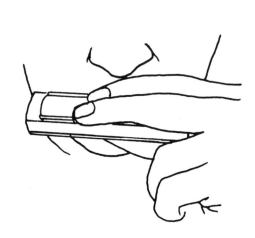

Left Hand　　　**Playing Position**　　　**Vibrato Position**

TYPES OF NOTES

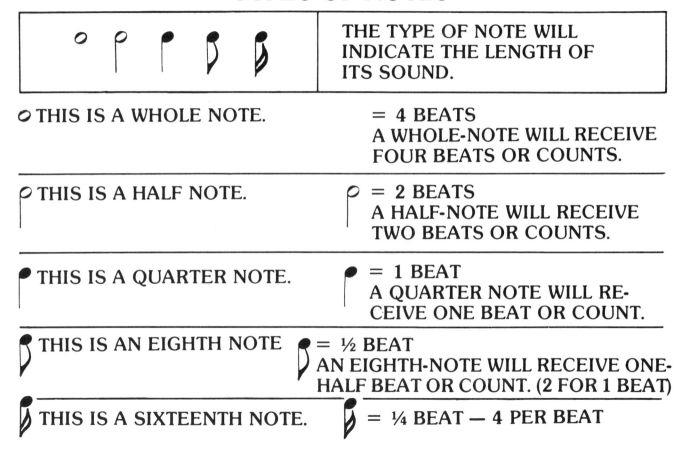

♩ ♩ ♩ ♪ ♪	THE TYPE OF NOTE WILL INDICATE THE LENGTH OF ITS SOUND.

THIS IS A WHOLE NOTE.

= 4 BEATS
A WHOLE-NOTE WILL RECEIVE FOUR BEATS OR COUNTS.

THIS IS A HALF NOTE.

= 2 BEATS
A HALF-NOTE WILL RECEIVE TWO BEATS OR COUNTS.

THIS IS A QUARTER NOTE.

= 1 BEAT
A QUARTER NOTE WILL RECEIVE ONE BEAT OR COUNT.

THIS IS AN EIGHTH NOTE

= ½ BEAT
AN EIGHTH-NOTE WILL RECEIVE ONE-HALF BEAT OR COUNT. (2 FOR 1 BEAT)

THIS IS A SIXTEENTH NOTE.

= ¼ BEAT — 4 PER BEAT

RESTS

A REST is a sign to designate a period of silence. This period of silence will be of the same duration as the note to which it corresponds.

𝄾 THIS IS AN EIGHTH REST   𝄽 THIS IS A QUARTER REST

𝄾 THIS IS A SIXTEENTH REST

▬ THIS IS A HALF REST
Note that it lays on the line.

▬ THIS IS A WHOLE REST
Note that it hangs down from the line.

NOTES

WHOLE 4 COUNTS	HALF 2 COUNTS	QUARTER 1 COUNT	EIGHTH 2 FOR 1 COUNT	SIXTEENTH 4 FOR 1 COUNT

RESTS

THE TIME SIGNATURE

The above examples are the common types of time signatures to be used in this book.

 $\frac{4}{4}$ The top number indicates the number of beats per measure

$\frac{4}{4}$ The bottom number indicates the type of note receiving one beat beats per measure

$\frac{4}{4}$ beats per measure

$\frac{4}{4}$ a quarter-note receives one beat.

$\frac{6}{8}$ BEATS PER MEASURE

EACH EIGHTH-NOTE RECEIVES ONE FULL BEAT
(See p. 26 & 27)

 Signifies so called "common time" and is simply another way of designating $\frac{4}{4}$ time.

PLAYING ONLY ONE NOTE

(Tone Blocking)

There are two ways of Blocking out undesired extra notes. One way is with the lips. With this technique the Harp player simply purses his lips so that only one tone sounds. This method can restrict your technique a bit later on. The best and most difficult method is by "Tongue Blocking." With this method your tongue covers and blocks off the three undesired holes on the left . While this method takes a degree of patience to learn, it is preferable, especially for Blues.

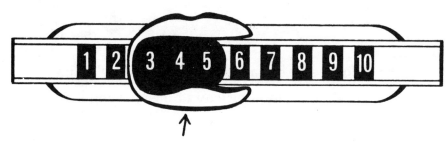

Tongue Blocks 3 holes,
Fourth hole sounds.

DIATONIC NOTE CHART

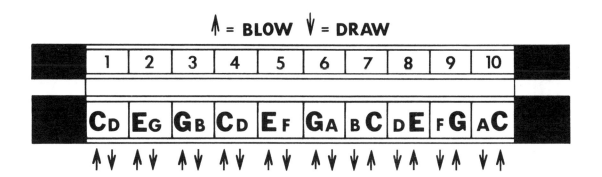

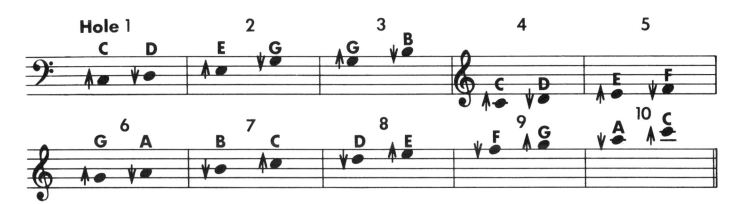

ACCOMPANIMENT CHORD TRANSPOSITION CHART

ACCOMPANIMENT CHORDS

	HARMONICA KEY											
	C	C# or Db	D	D# or Eb	E	F	F# or Gb	G	G# or Ab	A	A# or Bb	B
	C	Db	D	Eb	E	F	Gb	G	Ab	A	Bb	B
	C7	Db7	D7	Eb7	E7	F7	Gb7	G7	Ab7	A7	Bb7	B7
	F	Gb	G	Ab	A	Bb	B	C	Db	D	Eb	E
	G	Ab	A	Bb	B	C	Db	D	Eb	E	F	Gb
	G7	Ab7	A7	Bb7	B7	C7	Db7	D7	Eb7	E7	F7	Gb7
	Dm	Ebm	Em	Fm	Gbm	Gm	Abm	Am	Bbm	Bm	Cm	Dbm
	Am	Bbm	Bm	Cm	Dbm	Dm	Ebm	Em	Fm	Gbm	Gm	Abm
	Em	Fm	Gbm	Gm	Abm	Am	Bbm	Bm	Cm	Dbm	Dm	Ebm
	E7	F7	Gb7	G7	Ab7	A7	Bb7	B7	C7	Db7	D7	Eb7
	D7	Eb7	E7	F7	Gb7	G7	Ab7	A7	Bb7	B7	C7	Db7
	A7	Bb7	B7	C7	Db7	D7	Eb7	E7	F7	Gb7	G7	Ab7
	B7	C7	Db7	D7	Eb7	E7	F7	Gb7	G7	Ab7	A7	Bb7
	F#°	G°	Ab°	A°	Bb°	B°	C°	Db°	D°	Eb°	E°	F°
	F#7	G7	Ab7	A7	Bb7	B7	C7	Db7	D7	Eb7	E7	F7
	C°	Db7	D7	Eb7	E7	F7	Gb7	G7	Ab7	A7	Bb7	B7
	Fma7	Gbma7	Gma7	Abma7	Ama7	Bbma7	Bma7	Cma7	Dbma7	Dma7	Ebma7	Ema7

TIS SO SWEET

Gospel Song

↑ = Blow
↓ = Draw

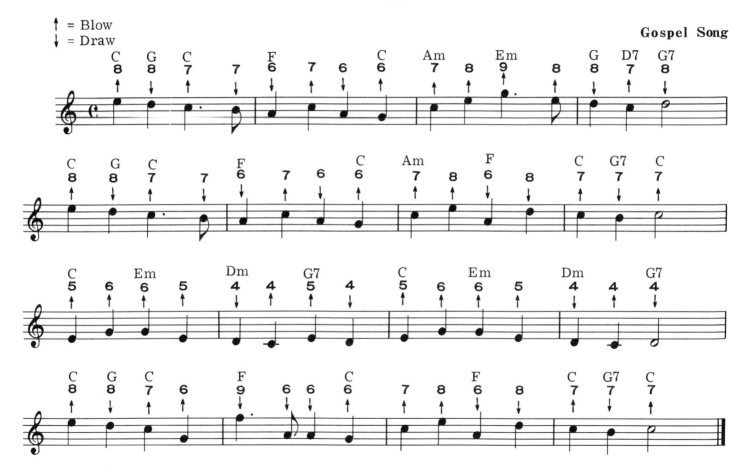

I NEED THEE EVERY HOUR

Gospel Song

STANDING ON THE PROMISES

↑ = Blow
↓ = Draw

Gospel Song

PRECIOUS MEMORIES

Gospel Song

NEAR THE CROSS

Gospel Song

BRINGING IN THE SHEAVES

Gospel Song

I'VE GOT PEACE LIKE A RIVER

THE LILY OF THE VALLEY

Gospel Song

↑ = Blow
↓ = Draw

Bright tempo

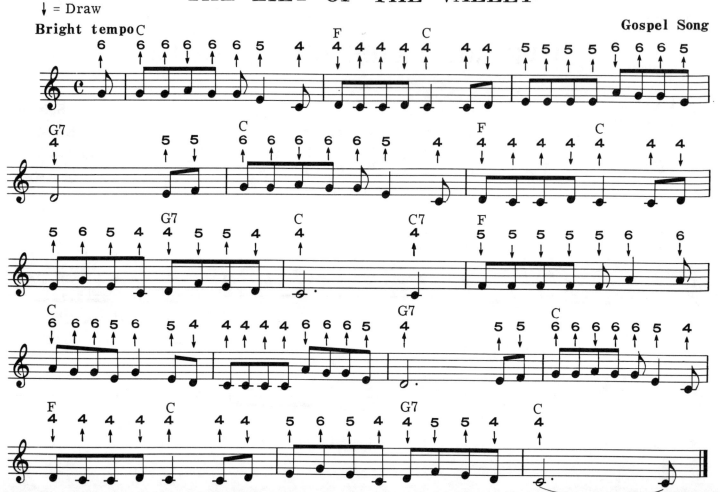

HIS BANNER OVER ME IS LOVE

Gospel Song

20

HOME ON THE RANGE

LORD, I'M COMING HOME

Gospel Song

↑ = Blow
↓ = Draw

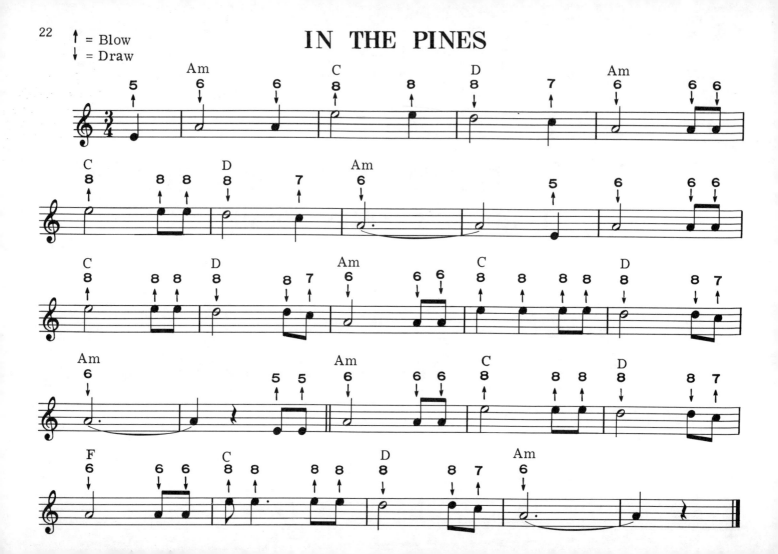

BLESSED BE THE NAME

Gospel Song

OLD ROSIN, THE BEAU

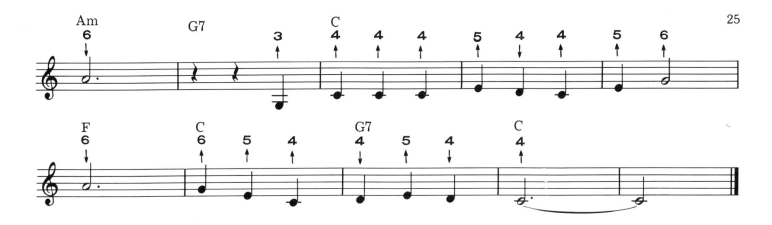

JESUS BREAKS EVERY FETTER

Gospel Song

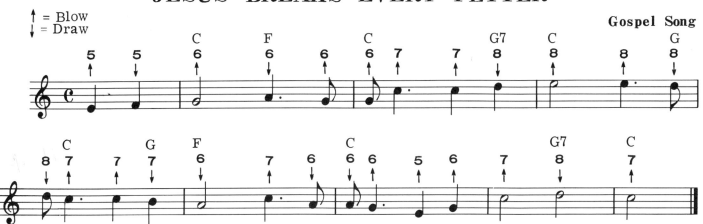

THE WEARIN' OF THE GREEN

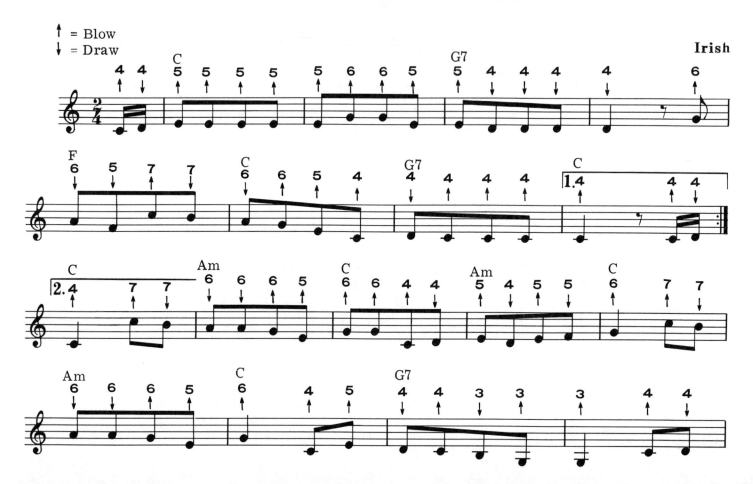

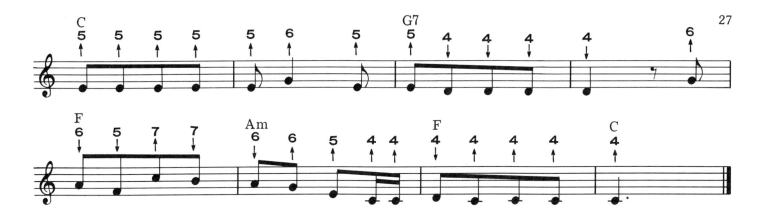

PRAISE HIM IN THE MORNING

↑ = Blow
↓ = Draw

Gospel Song

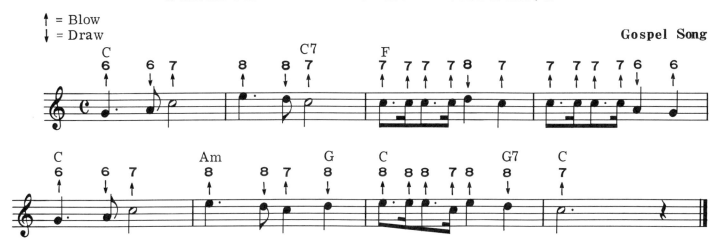

THE BATTLE CRY OF FREEDOM

THERE IS A TAVERN IN THE TOWN

↑ = Blow
↓ = Draw

NINE HUNDRED MILES

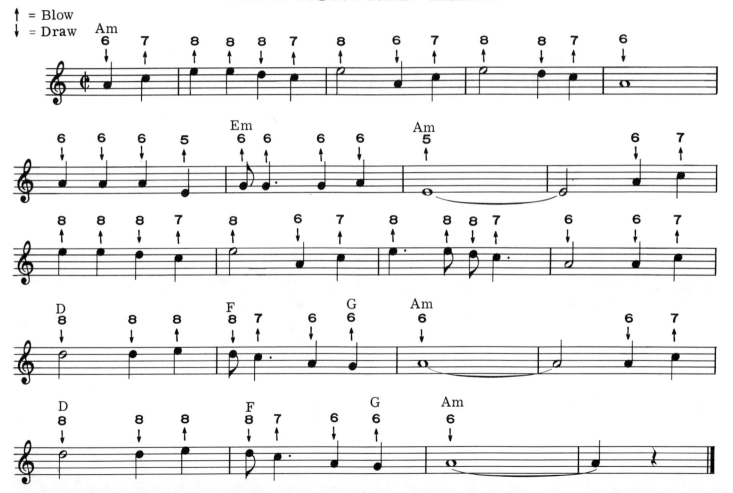

RAILROAD BILL

↑ = Blow
↓ = Draw

ROCK OF AGES

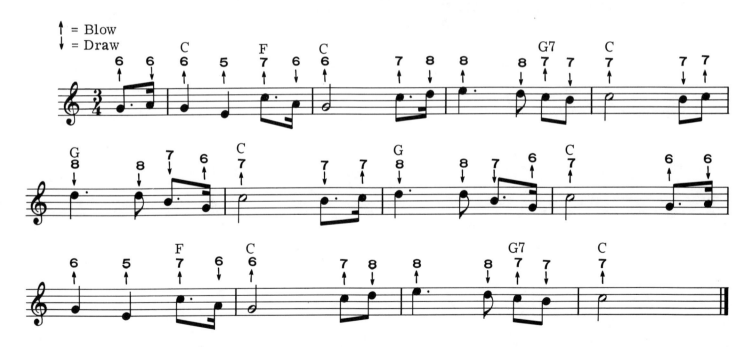

HOW FIRM A FOUNDATION

AMERICA THE BEAUTIFUL

BONNIE BLUE FLAG

COLUMBIA, THE GEM OF THE OCEAN

WE'RE MARCHING TO ZION

↑ = Blow
↓ = Draw

Chorus

AMERICA

HAUL AWAY JOE

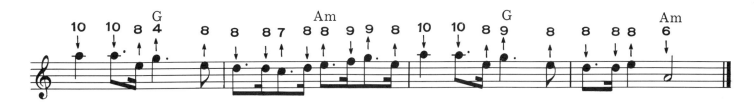

DOXOLOGY

REVIVE US AGAIN

TEN THOUSAND MILES

Scotch Song

↑ = Blow
↓ = Draw

GIVE ME OIL IN MY LAMP

HOW GREAT IS OUR GOD

↑ = Blow
↓ = Draw

Gospel Song

FOR HE'S A JOLLY GOOD FELLOW

46

↑ = Blow
↓ = Draw

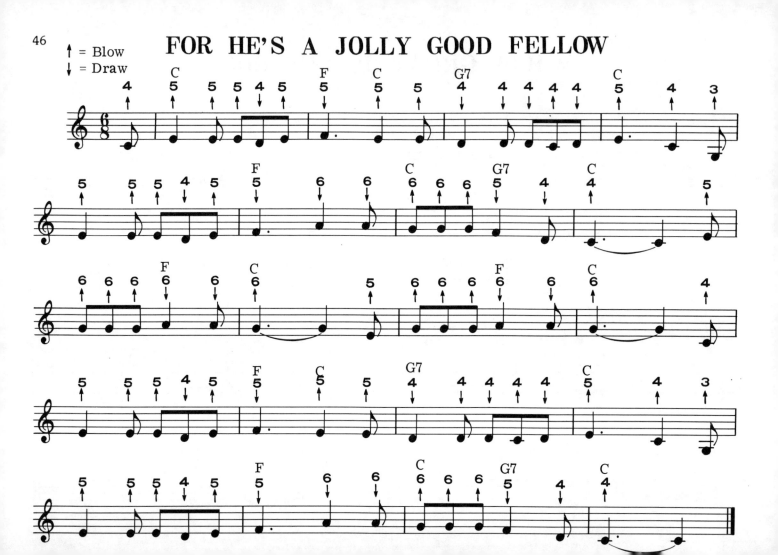

OUR BOYS WILL SHINE TONIGHT

TRAMP, TRAMP, TRAMP
(The Boys Are Marching)

MAMA DON'T 'LOW

DOWN BY THE RIVERSIDE

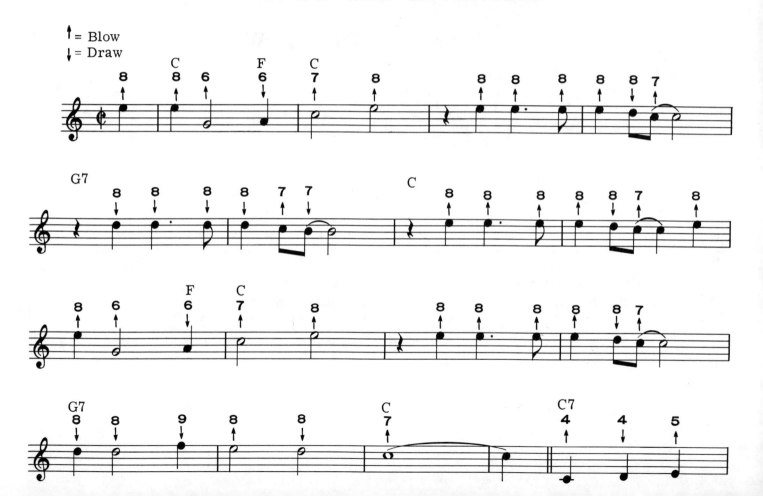

51

COMIN' THROUGH THE RYE

I KNOW WHERE I'M GOIN'

Scotch

↑ = Blow
↓ = Draw

THE BRITISH GRENADIERS

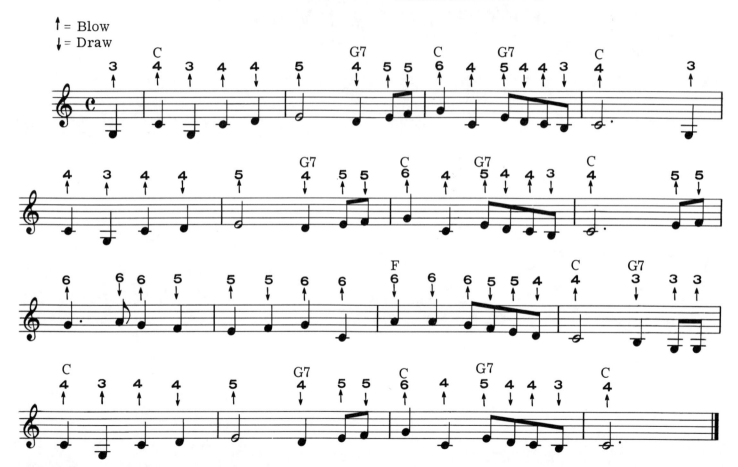

GOIN' DOWN THE ROAD FEELIN BAD

↑ = Blow
↓ = Draw

EVERYBODY LOVES SATURDAY NIGHT

SHE'LL BE COMIN' ROUND THE MOUTAIN

ROCK-A-MY SOUL

LORD LOVEL

English

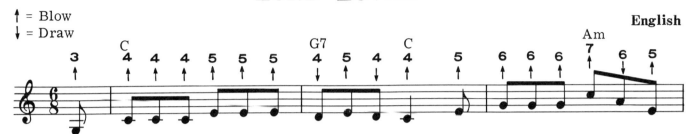

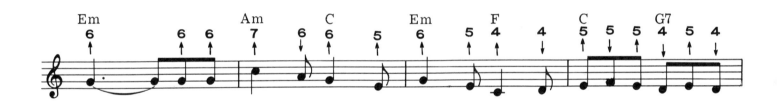

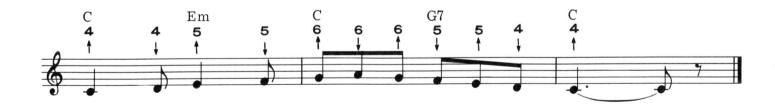

LOCH LOMOND

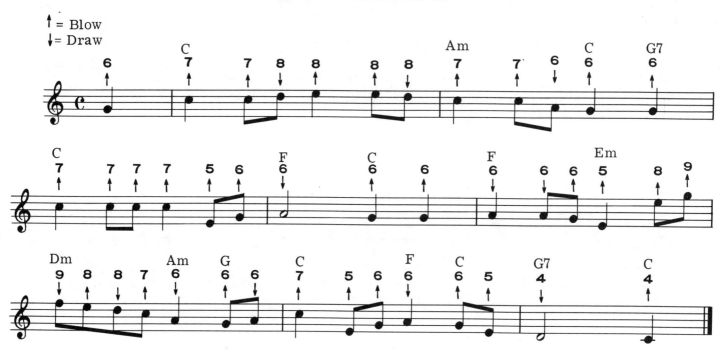

THE CAMPBELLS ARE COMIN'

Scotch

↑ = Blow
↓ = Draw

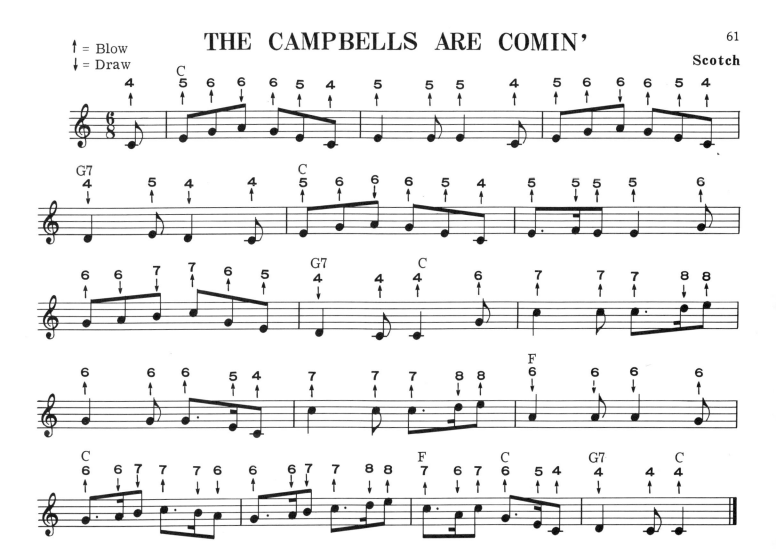

HEY LOLLY

↑ = Blow
↓ = Draw

ONCE THERE WERE THREE FISHERMAN

↑ = Blow
↓ = Draw

64

FATHER'S WHISKERS

RAISE A RUCKUS TONIGHT

↑ = Blow
↓ = Draw

MY HOME'S ACROSS THE SMOKEY MOUNTAINS

↑ = Blow
↓ = Draw

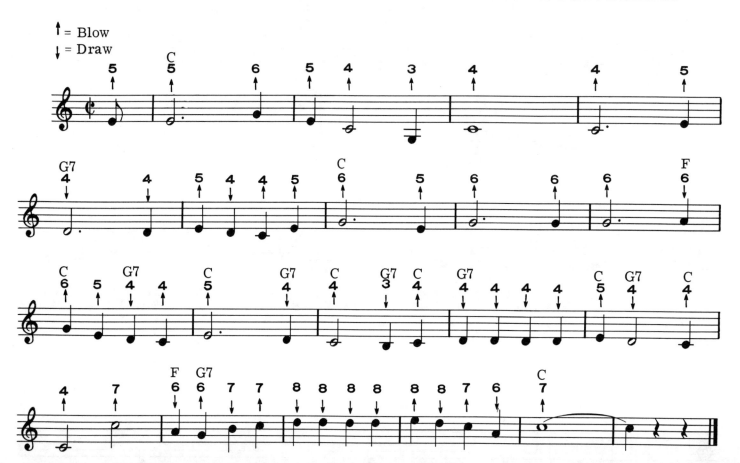

RISE & SHINE

↑ = Blow
↓ = Draw

PUTTING ON THE STYLE

THE ROVING GAMBLER

THE CAISSONS

NINE MEN SLEPT IN A BOARDING HOUSE

↑ = Blow
↓ = Draw

ONWARD CHRISTIAN SOLDIERS

GO IN AND OUT THE WINDOW

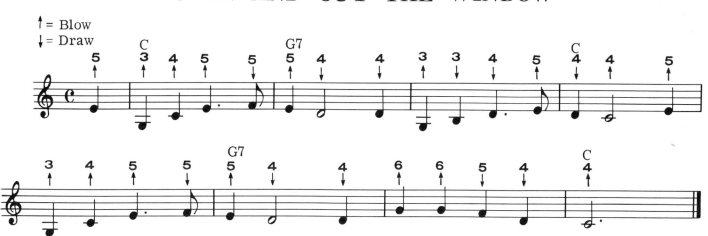

THE KEEPER

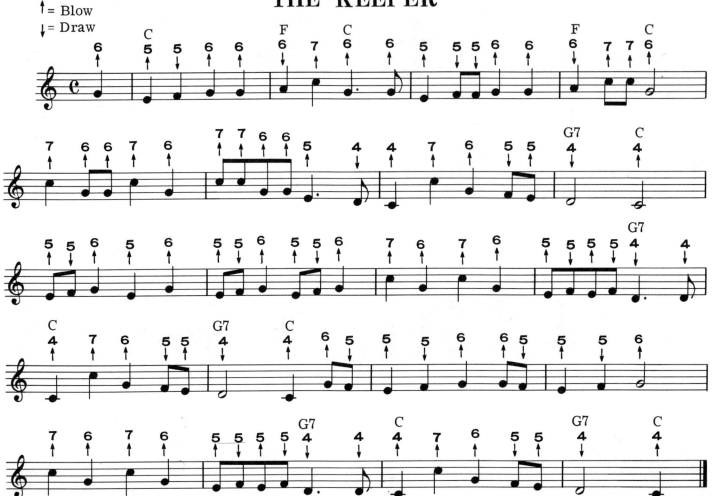

THE MULLIGAN GUARD

ON TOP OF OLD SMOKEY

Kentucky Mountain Song

THE MERMAID

American Sailing Song

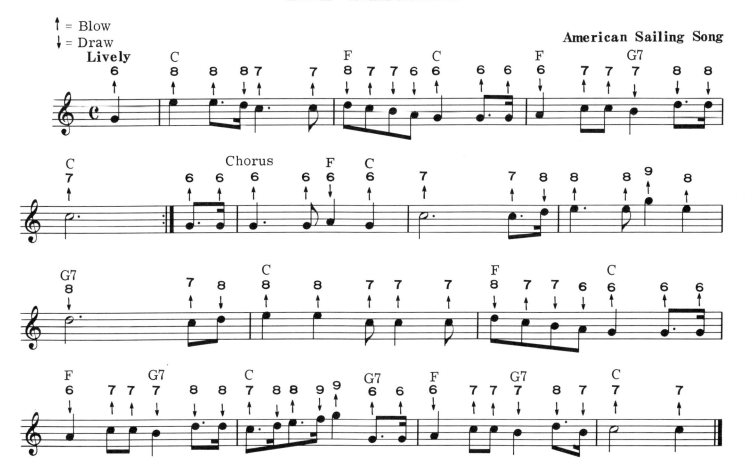

UP IN A BALLOON

MANDY LEE

↑ = Blow
↓ = Draw

American Ballad

↑ = Blow
↓ = Draw

DAISY BELL

STRIKE UP THE BAND

↑ = Blow
↓ = Draw

DUNDERBECK'S MACHINE

THE GIRL I LEFT BEHIND ME

83

↑ = Blow
↓ = Draw

THERE'S NO PLACE LIKE HOME

LOLLY TOO DUM

THIS LITTLE LIGHT OF MINE

↑ = Blow
↓ = Draw

SILVER THREADS AMONG THE GOLD

88

GRANDFATHER'S CLOCK

THE TEXAS RANGERS

90

REVILLE

↑ = Blow
↓ = Draw

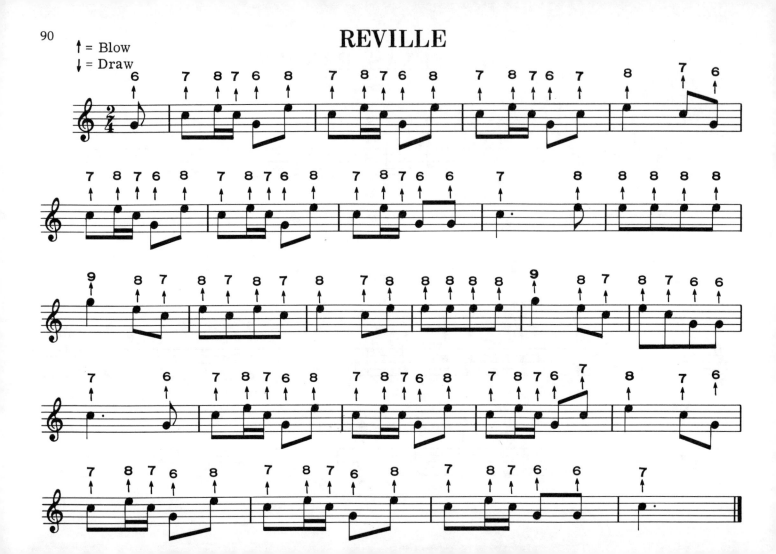

RED RIVER VALLEY

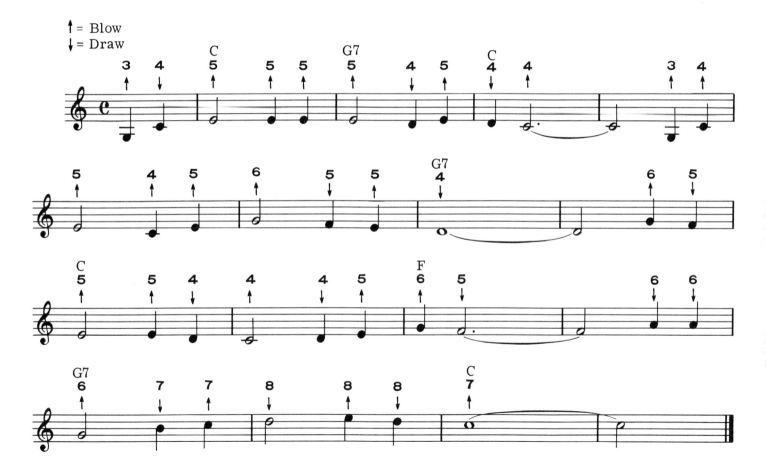

OLD COWBOY SONG

YELLOW ROSE OF TEXAS

SWEET BETSY FROM PIKE

Western Song

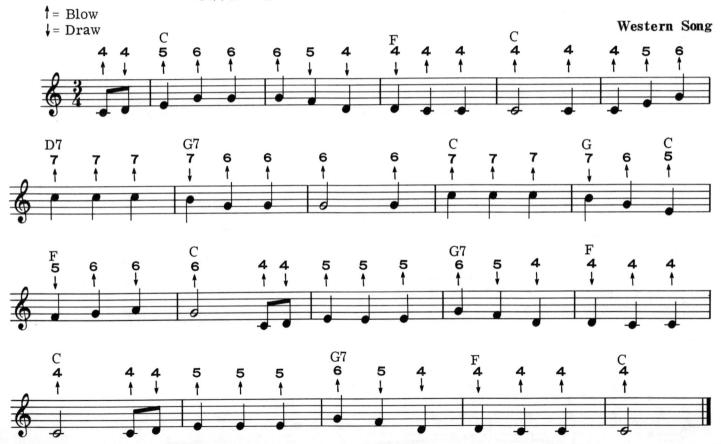

ALL GOD'S CHILDREN GOT SHOES

SWANEE RIVER

↑ = Blow
↓ = Draw

DIXIE

98

↑ = Blow
↓ = Draw

BUFFALO GALS

GIVE ME THAT OLD TIME RELIGION

↑ = Blow
↓ = Draw

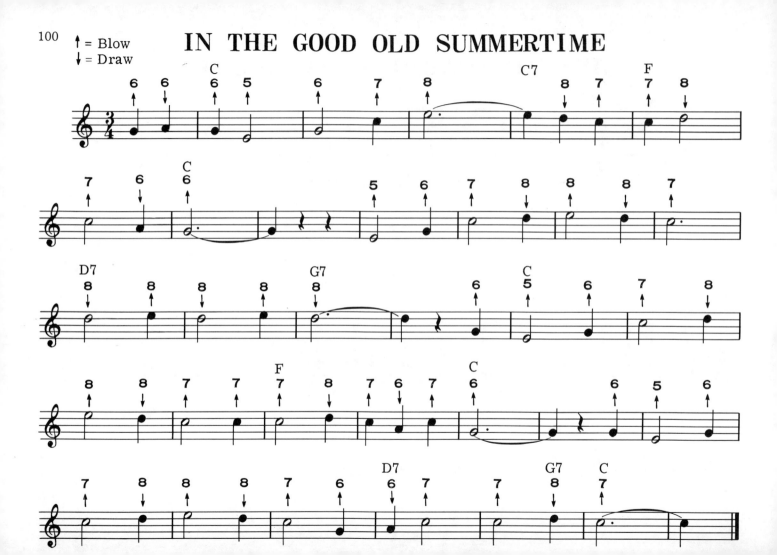

IN THE GOOD OLD SUMMERTIME

SHE WORE A YELLOW RIBBON

↑ = Blow
↓ = Draw

MARINES' HYMN

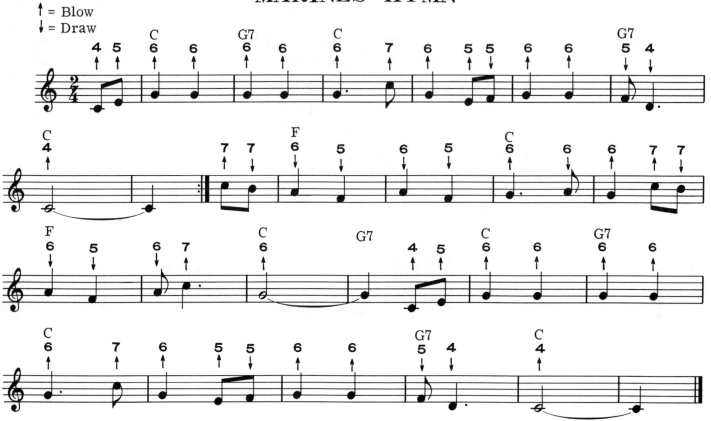

FAR ABOVE CAYUGA'S WATERS

EYES OF TEXAS

JOHN JACOB JINGLEHEIMER SCHMIDT

IRISH WASHERWOMAN

↑ = Blow
↓ = Draw

KOOKABURRA

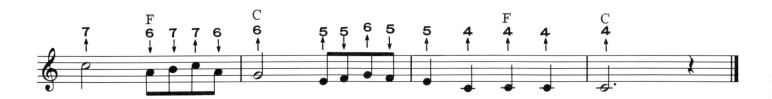

LITTLE BROWN JUG

108

MESS CALL

↑ = Blow
↓ = Draw

CZECH MARCHING SONG

↑ = Blow
↓ = Draw

SAILING SAILING

THERE ARE MANY FLAGS IN MANY LANDS

↑ = Blow
↓ = Draw

A CAPITAL SHIP

English

GERMAN FOLK SONG

FAREWELL TO SUMMER

↑ = Blow
↓ = Draw

HAIL TO THE CHIEF

↑ = Blow
↓ = Draw

THE HARP THAT ONCE THROUGH TARA'S HALLS

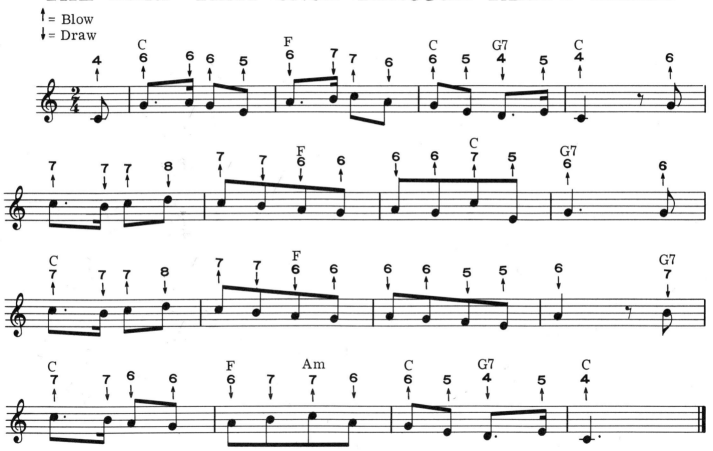

STEPHEN FOSTER SONG

DARLING NELLIE GREY

↑ = Blow
↓ = Draw

I WANT TO BE A SAILOR

Round

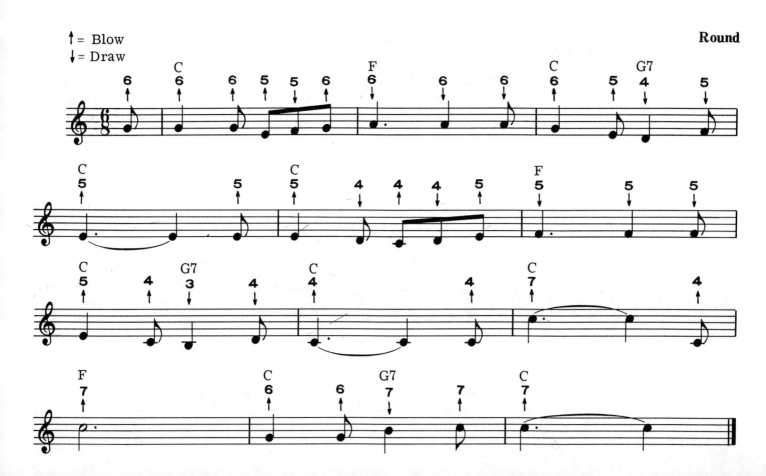

REUBEN AND RACHEL

↑ = Blow
↓ = Draw

THERE'S A HOLE IN MY BUCKET!

↑ = Blow
↓ = Draw

LITTLE DAVID PLAY ON YOUR HARP

↑ = Blow
↓ = Draw

Spiritual

IF YOU'RE HAPPY AND YOU KNOW IT

↑ = Blow
↓ = Draw

THE LAST ROSE OF SUMMER

Irish Ballad

DOWN WHERE THE COTTON BLOSSOMS GROW

↑ = Blow
↓ = Draw

Lively tempo

American Song

ASSEMBLY

↑ = Blow
↓ = Draw